Jackie Robinson

Speaks Out

Jackie Robinson

Speaks Out

Written & Narrated by

Don Mesibov

To my wife, Susan, and my children Raina, Marli, and Darren, and my daughter-in-law, Molly; and to my granddaughters Emelia, Avery, Madelyn, and Julia; the family that makes my happiness real and provides me the foundation that enables me to relax and write.

To my brother Gary, as ardent a Willie Mays fan as I was for Jackie Robinson.

To my late sister-in-law Laurie whose candor and encouragement are always with me.

Table of Contents

PART ONE: ARRANGING THE INTERVIEW

In the spring of 1947, Jackie Robinson became the first black player to take the field for a major league professional baseball club. In order to break the color barrier, he had to endure an ongoing barrage of verbal abuse, threats to his life, and the animosity of other players, some on his own team who demanded to be traded solely because of the color of his skin. Robinson's struggles to break baseball's color barrier have been well-documented in scores of books and at least two movies.

Brooklyn Dodger owner, Branch Rickey, signed Robinson to a minor league contract with the Montreal Royals, and Jackie played for a season in 1946. However, his experience in Montreal hardly prepared him for the vitriol, hate, and threats to his life that became part of his daily routine when he joined the major league club in the spring of 1947.

Robinson passed away in 1972 at the age of 52, and there are not a great many recordings of his actual voice. Unlike today when the media saturates us with information about any ballplayer who has one standout game, the coverage when Robinson played between 1947 and 1957 did not inundate sports fans with interviews and discussions of players' exploits. Therefore, much of what is available to baseball historians relate, as it should, only to Robinson's fight to break the color barrier and black-and-white videos of game footage. I want to offer a portrait of Jackie Robinson that is not available elsewhere. In this short book, I will share, in his own words, Jackie's views on a variety of topics, but leaving out what has been so frequently reported that you probably know it already or can find it with a quick google if you are interested in learning more about the actual events surrounding Robinson's breaking of the color barrier.

Five years after Jackie Robinson's retirement from baseball, I had the privilege of conducting an interview with this legendary human being. The interview was recorded for Boston University radio station WBUR and broadcast in its entirety only once – in the winter of 1962. A few excerpts from this interview were included on an episode of "The Story" on public radio a decade or two ago. In the entire interview, Jackie Robinson spoke out on his reaction to being elected to the Hall of Fame, his relationship with Branch Rickey, the man who chose Robinson as the person to break the color barrier, the art of stealing bases, particularly home plate, politics including why he supported Republican Richard Nixon over John F. Kennedy in the 1960 presidential election campaign, and the fight of Negroes, as African Americans were referred to then, to be treated like all other Americans.

This book is based on the interview I conducted with Jackie Robinson but also includes anecdotes related to my interview and people who interacted with Robinson.

So, how did I get the opportunity to interview my childhood idol? It started when I was barely seven years old. Each of the children in my neighborhood in Lynbrook, on Long Island, about a one-hour drive to Brooklyn, chose a team to root for and a player on that team to emulate. I chose Jackie Robinson probably because I was fascinated by the way he would dance off first base, daring the pitcher to try to pick him off. Or, maybe it was because my older cousin Fred suggested him in order to placate me since his favorite player was Duke Snider, and he wanted me to choose a different player. Either way, from that time on, Jackie was the one I watched and read about. I wore clothes with the number "42" and simply idolized him.

In the 1950s, the Dodgers played most of their games in the afternoon, and almost all games were televised. When they played a night game in Milwaukee, it would be at a time I was supposed to be in bed, so I would smuggle a portable radio under my pillow and listen to the play-by-play until the last out.

I remember one time when Robinson was on third base, and Leo Durocher, manager of the hated rival New York Giants, walked to the mound to talk with his pitcher. The TV announcer, probably Red Barber, proclaimed that Durocher was telling his pitcher to watch out for Robinson trying to steal home, a feat rarely attempted in baseball but patented by Robinson.

Durocher had barely crossed the third base line on his way back to the dugout when the pitcher went into his wind-up, and Robinson broke for home, beating the tag for one of the 19 times he successfully stole home during the regular season to go with his one swipe of home plate during a World Series, in 1955, when, according to the umpire, he slid under the tag by Yogi Berra. Berra demonstrated his disagreement with the call by jumping up and down and screaming in the face of the umpire. There were no instant replays in those days. You can access the play on YouTube and judge for yourself. But the umpire's decision will remain in the record books.

How well did I know Dem Bums as they were affectionally labeled by noted sports cartoonist Willard Mullin? Well, when the movie "42" was released in 2013, this excellent movie about Robinson's experiences breaking the color barrier had a scene with Gene Hermanski batting from the right side of the plate. Hermanski was a little-remembered outfielder who played for the Dodgers from 1943 to 1951. This surprised me because I knew Hermanski was a left-handed batter. I asked myself, "How could these movie makers who had paid scrupulous attention to detail in this film and probably even had a baseball expert on the set have possibly gotten this wrong?

Yet I was certain that Hermanski was a left-handed hitter, not right-handed, as portrayed in this film. A quick google search confirmed my recollection. Hermanski threw with the right hand, but he batted exclusively from the left side of the plate; he was neither a right-handed batter nor a switch hitter. My google search on Hermanski also uncovered a fact that I had not known, as quoted on page 62 of the book "Jackie Robinson," by Matt Christopher:

"When Hermanski played for the Brooklyn Dodgers along with Jackie Robinson, he demonstrated he was a great teammate by suggesting that all the players stand in solidarity by wearing Number 42 to confuse potential snipers who were said to be out to kill Robinson because he had broken the color barrier."

I should note that according to one source, Dodger shortstop Pee Wee Reese is credited with having said, at one time, "Maybe tomorrow we'll all wear number 42 so nobody can tell us apart." Of course, Reese and Hermanski were teammates, so perhaps each made a similar statement at one time or another.

A moment ago, I referred to Leo Durocher, known as "Leo the Lip," when he was managing the New York Giants. However, before going over to the Giants, Durocher was Dodger manager in 1946 when Robinson spent the baseball season with the Dodgers' minor league affiliate in Montreal and again in 1948. Durocher had been suspended in 1947 for, quote, "association with known gamblers." (Ironic now that major league baseball is currently encouraging gambling on games.) As Robinson's manager on the major league club in 1948, Durocher was asked about Robinson, and he said, "I don't care if the guy is yellow, or black, or if he has stripes like a F...in zebra. I'm the manager of this team, and I say he plays."

Unfortunately, not many of today's youth know much about this man, Jackie Robinson, who broke the color barrier in major league baseball – the man whose accomplishments on the field alone would have won him entrance to the select company of those outstanding ball players elected to the Hall of Fame in Cooperstown, but whose contributions toward achieving equal rights for people of color and other minorities overshadow his accomplishments on the ball field.

Not too long ago, I asked my granddaughter, nine years old at the time, what she knew about Jackie Robinson. "Who?" she responded. Even among students in the course I taught a few years ago at St. Lawrence University, less than half could identify Jackie Robinson. I had asked a randomly selected handful of my students, "Do you recognize the name Jackie Robinson and if so, what do you know about him?"

Many of my students, male and female, black and white, knew nothing more about Robinson than his name, and even among the ones who did know that he had broken the color barrier, few knew anything else about him.

Despite the wonderful documentary by Ken Burns and the day each year when Major League baseball honors Robinson by having every player wear his number 42 on their jerseys, along with the countless accolades publicized at benchmark anniversaries of the year 1947 when Robinson broke the color line, there is a need for this reminder of Robinson's contributions to all of us and to society in general.

Jackie is already a legend. Hopefully, I can add a little more to his well-earned legacy and, in doing so, remind us of what he fought for and how important it is that we continue the battle to eliminate discrimination of any kind in all walks of life.

Permit me a brief digression to demonstrate how times have changed with regard to gaining access to celebrities in contrast to the ease with which I was able to gain access to Jackie Robinson more than 60 years ago.

Trevor Noah, humorist and political commentator, formerly on Comedy Central, was appearing in Ottawa, Canada, a few years ago, and my wife Susan and I made the two-hour trip from our home in Northern New York to see him. I also wanted to share with him a book of poems by a local author who had written about her childhood experiences of being raised in poverty. I was certain if I could only get a copy to him, he would see the wisdom of promoting the book on his television show and possibly interviewing the author.

We arrived two hours before showtime and presented someone at the box office with a note in a thin envelope and asked if it could be delivered to Mr. Noah. We were told this was against the policy of the theater. A few years earlier, at this same theater, we were successful in getting a note delivered to Dionne Warwick. My wife's uncle had flown Ms. Warwick to her early concert performances, and when she received our note, she sent word that we could meet her backstage after the performance.

"Is there any way we can get a message to Mr. Noah?" I asked. "No," I was told.

We decided to wait outside to try to get his attention as he left the theater. But he was so closely protected from fans that it was impossible to get near him on his short journey from the theater exit to his chauffeured limousine.

In 1998, our two young daughters had gotten autographs from Bernadette Peters following her

Broadway appearance in Annie Get Your Gun by waiting outside the theater and catching her when she stopped to sign autographs. She graciously signed their programs. No such luck this time, and I do not intend this as a criticism of Trevor Noah as much as a sign of the security-conscious times in which we live.

Now let's flashback to January 25th, 1962. I was in my third year of college, the second year since transferring from Lehigh University, where I may have been the only student not majoring in engineering. When I came to the realization that I needed to pay more attention to preparing for a career, I chose Boston University because of the strength of its communications/public relations program. Upon taking residence in a dormitory on Beacon Hill, I began as a student reporter for WBUR, which at that time was a training vehicle for students at Boston University. By the following year, I had my own one-hour show in which I would interview people in the field of sports.

Second only to the interview with Robinson, my prized guest was Red Auerbach, who was coach of the

Boston Celtics and who, in those days, won more championships than not.

As I have indicated, since I was seven years old, my childhood idol has been Jackie Robinson. I had been a fanatical Brooklyn Dodger fan and watched almost every Dodger game during their 154-game schedule and, then, frequently, the World Series. In those days, there were no playoffs; there were two eight-team divisions, and whichever teams in the National and American Leagues won the most regular season games got to play in the World Series.

The Dodgers, beginning in 1947, were the first team to sign a black player to a major league contract. Robinson was the first, but he was quickly followed on the Dodgers by Roy Campanella, Joe Black, Don Newcombe, and Junior Gilliam, all of whom became the core of the most successful baseball team of the 1950s, with the exception only of the New York Yankees. Robinson was followed in July of 1947 by Larry Doby, who broke the color barrier in the American League when he was signed by the Cleveland Indians. Twelve years later, in 1959, the Boston Red Sox became the last of the sixteen major league clubs to integrate when they brought up Pumpsie Green from their minor league system.

Ironically, the Red Sox could have become the first, rather than the last, team to integrate. They gave Jackie Robinson a tryout in 1945, but despite a strong showing, they failed to offer him a contract. In baseball terms alone, this may have been one of the two biggest mistakes ever made by one team, the other being the sale of Babe Ruth to the Yankees in 1920. Imagine how the history of the Red Sox would be altered if the ball club could lay claim to the legacies of Babe Ruth and Jackie Robinson.

The Dodgers won pennants in 1947, 1952, 1953, 1955, and 1956, only to face the Yankees each of those years, and it was 1955 before they won their first World Series.

Here's a fun fact: Prior to 1955, since the first World Series game in 1903, there had been 51 World Series (skipping only 1904), and no team had ever lost the first two games and then come back to win the Series. In 1955, the Dodgers lost the first two games and then became the first team to overcome a 2-0 lead in games to win. The victory gave the Dodgers their first World Series success in the franchise's history, four games to three, and it was the eighth time the team had played in the Series since their founding in 1911.

The following year, 1956, the Yankees reversed the plot, losing the first two games to the Dodgers and then winning the Series 4 games to 3, including Don Larsen's perfect game, the only no-hitter ever pitched in a World Series by one person.

Two years in a row, the team that lost the first two games came back to win the World Series, something that hadn't been done in the previous 52 years.

Now back to my story: On January 23rd, 1962, it was announced that Jackie Robinson and Bob Feller had been elected to the Baseball Hall of Fame, and it was the first time that each had been eligible for election. Also, they were the first players to be elected during their first year of eligibility. Players cannot gain entry to the Hall until they have been retired for at least five years, and then they need to be elected during elections that take place annually.

Robinson retired in 1957 following the announcement that he had been traded to the rival San Francisco Giants. That was the year that Walter O'Malley and Horace Stoneman had transferred the Dodger and Giant franchises to Los Angeles and San Francisco, respectively. Robinson negated the trade by retiring. He said that he had already decided to retire but had withheld a formal announcement as part of an agreement with Look Magazine to allow them to have an exclusive story announcing his retirement.

In contrast to the difficulty of getting near celebrities in the 21st century, let me share how easy it was for me to interview Jackie Robinson: My roommate, Bob Dick, from Providence, Rhode Island, was also a fellow reporter for WBUR, the student radio station at that time. In those days, we used a reel-to-reel tape recorder to record interviews. The tape recorder was housed in a medium-sized suitcase-like enclosure, and the person who ran the tape recorder was called the engineer. As such, the engineer moves the dials to adjust the volume level and clarity.

It was our plan that if we could land any interviews, we would alternate between conducting an interview and acting as engineer for each other. Bob, knowing of my idolatry of Jackie Robinson, agreed that I could conduct the Robinson interview.

As it turned out, Bob didn't do too badly himself. Also attending the dinner were two Boston Red Sox players who had had excellent rookie seasons and were being touted as future stars, and Bob conducted interviews with each of them. One, second baseman Chuck Shilling, went on to have a non-descript career and was gone from the Red Sox within five years. The other was Carl Yastrzemski, who went on to play his entire 23-year career with the Sox and is in the Hall of Fame with Robinson.

Subsequent to the announcement of their election to the Hall, the Boston Baseball Writers announced they would honor Feller and Robinson at their annual dinner at the Boston Hilton Hotel on January 25th. Bob and I arrived at the hotel mid-afternoon, hours before the advertised start of the dinner. Finally, we spotted Robinson at the hotel registration desk along with a traveling companion who turned out to be his public relations representative.

We watched them register and then disappear into the elevator, waited approximately five minutes, and then I used the phone in the lobby to call their room. The hotel clerk had no problem connecting me. "I'm Don Mesibov with Boston University Radio, and I'd like to interview Mr. Robinson," I said to his companion, who had answered the phone. "One minute," he said, and then I could hear a brief discussion, not loud enough to distinguish what was being said. He returned to the phone and told me to "Come on up."

Jackie welcomed us graciously, and while Bob unhitched the cumbersome tape recorder from its casing, Jackie motioned toward the couch in the main room of his suite and asked if that would be a good place to conduct the interview.

In a few minutes, I was seated alongside my idol, the recorder on the floor in front of us, while Bob monitored sound levels by maintaining vigilant attention to the dial on the tape recorder's platform.

I began the interview with an exaggerated excitement in my voice that was my impression of how leading sportscasters of the time sounded, and then I dived right into the first question.

PART TWO: ROBINSON SPEAKS OF HIS ELECTION TO THE BASEBALL HALL OF FAME IN COOPERSTOWN, NEW YORK.

Don: It's been speculated in the newspapers for a long time that you would be elected to the Hall of Fame, and you've won many awards in your baseball career; was this just another award to you? Did you take this in stride?

Jackie: It's impossible to take an honor such as this in stride, Don. I was thrilled. We've been up on cloud nine for about 48 hours, and I don't know when we're coming down. It's just a tremendously wonderful feeling, and I'm thrilled beyond words, and I'm very appreciative of the things that have happened to me over the last few years.

Don: When was the first time you started to think seriously about the possibility you might someday be elected to the Hall of Fame?

Jackie: I would have to say, in all honesty, just recently because I didn't really give a great deal of thought to it, not even when I retired from baseball because first, you have to wait a five-year period, then I started looking around and noticing how long it took some of the real greats of baseball to get into the Hall of Fame and I wasn't going to be disappointed personally if I didn't get in.

So I just sort of took it in stride, and it was only until the last month and a half or so that I really started to think about it because newspapermen started calling and asking me questions; how I would feel if I got in, or how I would feel if I didn't get in. And I gave it a little thought. I talked it over with my family. But, as I say, I had built up a little shield for myself personally, so if I didn't get in, I wouldn't be too disappointed.

Don: Supposedly, the first person you called when you heard you had been elected was Branch Rickey. Was this only because he was the man who

gave you the opportunity to break into baseball, or was there more to it?

Jackie: There's a lot more to it than that, Don. Mr. Rickey has been somewhat like a father to me. I put in two calls at about the same time. The first one went to my mother. My wife was sitting alongside me, so I didn't have to call her. My first call went to my mother, and the line was busy. So I waited a couple of minutes and called her back; it was still busy, so I then put in a call to Mr. Rickey. I wanted to be the one to pass it along. I did this because it's impossible to estimate what Mr. Rickey meant to me and my career, what he meant to the early days of my baseball. Had it not been for the constant advice, guidance, and inspiration that he gave me, I couldn't even have been given consideration for going into the Hall of Fame. So in my thinking, when I heard the news, the first people that came to my mind were Mr. Rickey and my mother, and I felt I had to call them immediately because I felt it was their honor as well as mine.

Dodger's owner Branch Rickey said of Robinson: "There was never a man in the game who could put mind and muscle together quicker and with better judgment than Jackie Robinson." About Robinson joining the Dodgers in 1947, Rickey said, "We've got no army. There's virtually nobody on our side. No owners, no umpires, and very few newspapermen. And I'm afraid that many fans will be hostile. We'll be in a tough position. We can win only if we can convince the world that I'm doing this because you're a great ballplayer, a fine gentleman."

Robinson once said of Rickey: "The thing about him was that he was always doing something for someone else. I know because he did so much for me."

Jackie Robinson won the very first Rookie of the Year award (an award later renamed the Jackie Robinson Award in his honor). While Robinson only played Major League baseball for ten years, he led the Brooklyn Dodgers to six pennants and finished with a career batting average of .311.

Robinson was a natural second baseman, but he began his Brooklyn career at first base since the Dodgers already had a regular second baseman, Eddie Stanky. Stanky is alleged to have told Robinson, upon their first meeting in the spring of 1947 when Robinson joined the major league club, that he was not in favor of integrating baseball and that he was unhappy that it was his own team doing it, but that despite his own personal feelings, Robinson was now his teammate, and Stanky promised he would have his back. However, following the '47 season, Stanky was traded to the Boston Braves, and Robinson became the Dodgers' regular second baseman, a position he played for most of his career.

PART THREE: STEALING HOME PLATE

Don: Jackie, you played many positions during your career: first base, second base, third base, and left field. Which did you enjoy the most? And which did you find most difficult?

Jackie: Well, I enjoyed playing second base because I knew how to play that position best. I started in Montreal at second base, and I played one year at first base at the start of a season, and that was tough for me. But when I moved to second base, I became relaxed and at ease. Then I moved over to third when I got to be a little older. Then I got another year older, so they moved me to left field, and that was really tough. I couldn't play the outfield. I remember trying to run in on a ball in Philadelphia. I was coming in fast, and I was running on my heels, and all of a sudden, it looked like the ball was bouncing up and down, and when I finally got to it, I reached for it, and when I thought it was down, actually it was up and when it went by it just barely missed hitting me on the top of the head. So I figured that left field was the toughest position because I wasn't an outfielder, and any baseball player will tell you that when you don't know anything about a position, it's really tough trying to move in and play it and play it well.

As a footnote to Jackie's response, in 1951, his seven errors were, at the time, a record for the fewest errors by a second baseman in a single 154-game season.

Perhaps explaining how his inexperience with fly balls hindered his ability to play left field, Robinson once said, "Pop flies are just a diversion for a second baseman; grounders are his stock and trade."

Early on, I decided to ask about the aspect of his game I personally enjoyed the most: base running.

Don: Jackie, you were one of the examples of the truly all-around ball player – base running, hitting,

and fielding. Of these three, which did you enjoy the most?

Jackie: Oh, I liked running the bases. That was a big thrill. I could always tell when I had the opposition somewhat rattled, and when I ran, and they were rattled, I got a big kick out of it, and I tried to carry it on.

I often marveled how some of the guys would get so upset that instead of throwing the ball at the plate, they would have much preferred to have thrown it at me. And I remember one time when I was stealing home, the pitcher was so angry he didn't even come close to home plate, he threw the ball right at me, and I slid in without any chance of being out. The ball went up against the railing in the back, and I got up kind of laughing, inwardly, because the fellow had been tremendously upset, and he couldn't do anything other than throw the ball at me.

And sometimes, it would upset the whole team to the point where we were able to go on and win games. And I loved that part of it. I liked all of baseball when I was playing, but base stealing was the number one thing for me.

Don: Jackie, I'm glad to hear you say that because I think that's what the fans found most exciting, also. How do you go about stealing home plate?

Jackie: Well, actually, it's reflexes. You can't make up your mind on any given pitch that you're going to try to steal home because you can't outrun the baseball. But when you're moving up and down the line, the first thing I knew I had to do was get well off of third base before the pitcher even started his motion, and when he started, I had to make my move immediately, and if it appeared to me that he was going to stop at the height of his wind-up, that's when your reflexes came in, and you have to go on home real quick, or you have to break yourself and go on back. So it's reflexes, and you couldn't say on any given pitch, "Well, I'm going home on this particular pitch," because it depended on what the pitcher was doing on the mound.

Don: When actually, then, did you make up your mind to go home?

Jackie: It had to be the last split second; if I got about halfway home and it appeared to me the pitcher was going to throw home, I would stop and dart back as fast as I could because if I didn't get back real quick I would be thrown out at third base and certainly I'd be out by a quarter of the way if he started to throw when I was halfway; so I would have to be almost three-quarters of the way down the line before I decided that I was going to go.

It seems almost an impossible thing to say, but when I started with the 90-foot line, I knew I had to be at least 30 feet up the baseline before I knew I could even attempt it, and I would move up another third or fourth of the way before I knew that I had a chance of going home. And then, in many cases, I was safe only because the pitcher threw the ball a little too high or he made a bad toss at the plate, and the catcher had to go out to get the ball. So it's a most difficult thing, the steal of home, but it was exciting to me, as it was to the fans.

Robinson's record of successfully stealing home 19 times (or 61% of his attempts) is ninth on the all-time list, tied with Frankie Frisch, nicknamed The Fordham Flash, who played from 1919 until 1937. However, his 19 successful swipes of home plate lead all modern-day players. Each of the other eight players who stole home 19 or more times began their baseball careers prior to 1920. Only Rod Carew, with 17, and Paul Molitor, with 10, even approach Robinson's record for players in the post second world war era.

More impressive is that all of Robinson's steals of home were straight steals where he broke for home as the pitcher was into his wind-up and either beat the throw to home plate or slid under the catcher's tag. While today's players occasionally steal home, often it is on a strategic play wherein a runner on first base breaks for second, and when the catcher throws to second, the runner on third breaks for home and, if successful, is credited with a steal of home.

To put Robinson's feat in perspective, consider these purported facts from Wikipedia:

- In the past 100 years, only 30 players have been successful with a straight steal of home plate.
- The last time anyone stole home was in 1996 when Eric Young Sr. stole second, third, and home in the same inning, according to Baseball Almanac.
- The last person to steal home plate in a World Series game was Jackie Robinson in 1955.

Before leaving Robinson's base running exploits, we would be remiss if we didn't comment on his ability to escape a rundown. This was truly a unique feat mainly because baseball players are rarely successful at avoiding a tag once they are caught in a rundown between bases, and, in fact, some players, when caught in a rundown, simply give up and start walking toward the dugout before they are even tagged. Yet, as much traveled manager Bobby Bragan, a contemporary of Robinson's, observed, "He was the only player I ever saw caught in a rundown who could be safe more often than out. He ran as if his head was on a swizzle, back and forth, back and forth, until he could get out of it."

My recollection is that in addition to his swizzling back and forth, back and forth, Robinson employed lightning-quick reflexes, and he utilized a rule that many of today's players probably don't even realize exists. A defensive player can only be in the baseline if he is holding the ball when a runner runs into him. Robinson would let the defensive player run him toward a base, but the moment the player let the ball out of his hands, thinking Robinson was making a dash for the base ahead of him, Robinson would turn on a dime and run into the player who had just released the ball. The umpire would call interference and award Robinson the base he was headed toward when he ran into the person who had just thrown the ball.

Don: Who was the toughest pitcher to steal a base off?

Jackie: Well, when you start from first base, Warren Spahn was the toughest pitcher. I never tried to steal on Warren because I remember too frequently being hung up between first and second with egg on my face with Spahn, and I decided if I got on base against Warren Spahn, I was going to stay there, and he wasn't going to pick me off because the longest walk of any I know other than that of being taken out as far as a pitcher is concerned is when you get thrown out being picked off a base, and the umpire says "out," and you have to go from second base all the way into the dugout. It's like you just wanted to dig a hole and crawl under the ground and go in there.

But to me, Warren Spahn had the greatest move of any I know. Right-handers; there were a number of them with great moves. They would give you deception by dropping that left leg down, and the next thing you'd know, that ball is coming to first, but of all the ones I know, I would pick Warren Spahn in the National League.

In 1947, 'Dem Bums,' as the Brooklyn Dodgers were lovingly called, made it to the World Series after their best season ever, although they lost the Series to the Yankees in seven games.

1949, statistically, was Robinson's best season, hitting .342 with 124 RBIs; he led the league with 37 stolen bases and was named the National League's Most Valuable Player. Based on his 1949 performance, in 1950, he received a $35,000 salary, the highest in Dodger history and a substantial increase from the $5,000 salary he received three years earlier in 1947, his first year in the major leagues.

Don: I think you've said before that 1951 was your most exciting season or the season where you thought you contributed the most to the Dodgers. And yet, in 1949, you hit .342 and won the batting

crown. You also knocked in 124 RBIs as compared with 88 in 1951, and in other statistics, you were better in 1949. Why, then, was 1951 a better season for you?

Jackie: Well, I'm a guy that does not believe in statistics. I don't think they really tell a man's value to his ball team. A guy hits 35 home runs, but he hits them when they don't mean a thing. A guy hits .324 but doesn't get the hit at the proper time. I felt that perhaps I didn't know what the statistics were; as I said, they don't mean very much- but I thought that in '51, I got more key hits to help our ball club than I did -you say I had 124 RBI's in '49- I feel that I got more key hits in '51 then I did in '49, and my contributions to the ball club were greater in my opinion.

Continuing on our journey down memory lane, I asked Jackie Robinson,

Don: If you could see a film of one game the Dodgers played during your career, which game do you think you'd pick?

Jackie: That's a difficult question. It certainly wouldn't be the Giant game of 1951; I assure you of that.

I think it would have to be the last game of the 1955 World Series. Although I was sitting on the bench watching the ball game, I can picture today Sandy Amoros going over and making the great catch and turning it into a double play. I can picture the last play of the ball game as Reese catches the ball and throws it to Gil Hodges. I can remember darting out of the dugout to join in the jubilation. This is the game I want to remember most of all the games that I've ever participated in or had anything to do with.

It was a tremendous feeling because, for baseball players, winning the World's Championship is something that you just hope for all along, and after facing the Yankees in four previous years and not winning and finally beating them on the fifth try gave me a great thrill.

One of the saddest memories of my childhood occurred at 3:58 pm on Wednesday, October 3rd, 1951. This was the date of the game Robinson had in mind when he said, "It certainly wouldn't be the Giant game of 1951." It was a month and a half before my tenth birthday. I had arrived home from school, and my mother had the television turned to the deciding playoff game between the Dodgers and the Giants. The teams had split the previous two games, and the winner would go to the World Series.

I was still standing by the TV with my coat on as Ralph Branca came in to pitch for the Dodgers in the last of the ninth inning with Brooklyn leading 4 to 2. This was the day of Bobby Thompson's 'Shot heard 'Round the World,' when the New York Giants outfielder hit a three-run homer to give the Giants the pennant and a trip to the World Series. I stood stone-faced, mouth open in disbelief.

I took Jackie back to that 1951 season, but I wasn't going to rehash the final playoff game. Instead, I wanted him to reflect on a sensational play he had made during the last weekend of the regular 1951 season when his heroics made it possible for the Dodgers to tie the Giants and get into the playoff.

"The Dodgers began the final game of the regular season tied with the Giants for first place," I reminded him. "The Giants' victory over the Braves, 3-2, behind Larry Jansen had already been posted on the scoreboard, and the Dodgers needed to win, or their season would be over. The Dodgers made up deficits of 6-1 to the Phillies and then 8-5.

It was a tie score heading into the bottom of the eleventh inning in Philadelphia. The bases were loaded with two outs, and the Phillies' Eddie Waitkus hit a line drive," I continued prefacing my question to Jackie Robinson. "The radio announcer had already screamed that it was into right field and the Giants had won the pennant when he suddenly reversed himself and said that Jackie Robinson had made a sensational diving catch. And then he said that you flipped the ball to Reese at second to get the force just in case the umpire ruled your catch a trap.

"Now, in a Long Island newspaper, Newsday, about a year ago, Jack Mann (whom I mistakenly referred to as Jack Lang in the interview) claimed that you had definitely trapped the ball, but that being the great competitor you were, and being smart, you had stayed on the ground on top of the ball knowing that the umpire would not want to rule it safe and end the pennant on a call he couldn't be sure of.

Don: Jackie, what was the truth? Did you catch the ball? Was there a flip to Reese at second base?

Jackie: I caught the ball at least a foot off the ground; in my opinion, it was that high off the ground. I flipped the ball to second base just before I felt myself going out. I jammed my elbows into my ribs. I don't know where Jack was at that particular time to say that I had trapped the ball, but he certainly wasn't in any position to see it. Jocko Conlon (the umpire) was right on top of the play.

There was no doubt in his mind about my catching it. There has never been any doubt in my mind about catching that ball, and I can imagine that whoever wrote this, you say, Jack Mann, I would imagine Jack was probably sitting in Long Island, and the game was being played in Philadelphia if he made that statement.

Lang was a well-respected sports reporter who enjoyed a distinguished career. While I had mistakenly referred to him as Jack Mann, I believe my characterization of that article was correct. Incidentally, in addition to Robinson's game-saving catch in the bottom of the 11th inning, he hit the game-winning home run in the top of the 14th inning to give the Dodgers the tie for the pennant that sent them into the three-game playoff series with the Giants.

"Well," I affirmed, "I guess that rather emphatically settles the issue."

Don: Jackie, was there ever any time that you went up to home plate and that you had it set in your mind that you wanted to hit a home run?

Jackie: Well, I was a kind of a baseball player that knew that if I went up to home plate with it on my mind that I was going to hit a home run or attempt a homerun at this time that I was a dead pigeon because I wasn't a home run hitter and I knew that if the only way that I could hit a home run was that in my swing, which was one that came down from up high, I hadn't held my bat very high, that I would just get under the ball just a wee bit more than I usually did and the ball would, with the spin, would carry a long way. But most of the time, I hit line drives. I knew it, and I never went for a home run except when the game was out of the question or some such thing like that. If I attempted to do this, I usually popped it, and I could see the catcher catching these balls every time I attempted to hit a home run. So I knew this wasn't for me, and I would just try to meet the ball and let it do whatever it would.

While Jackie Robinson was not known as a homerun hitter, neither was he what could be called a light hitter. Throughout his ten year career he averaged 14 homeruns a year, and 76 RBIs.

Don: How about the players of today? Do you think there is a tendency or a trend for them to try for the home run instead of hitting it where it's pitched?

Jackie: I think Maris is, yes, perhaps because that's the kind of swinger he is. Mantle is a hard, free swinger. I certainly think that a guy like Nelly Fox, for instance, would be a real one; it would be ridiculous for him to walk up and try to hit a home run. Aparicio, I'm sure that there are guys on the Boston Ball Club that are the same way that is line drive hitters, are singles, and doubles and triples hitters.

It would be ridiculous for them to go up and attempt to hit home runs. Each of us has to know our capabilities. Each of us will have to know how we swing. I think this is true in baseball; it's true in business. You have to know your capabilities, and if you're not a home run hitter, I would say certainly don't go up there trying to hit the home run, or you'll find yourself doing nothing but making big outs.

One of the thoughts I had over the years is about how thin the line is between someone being a hero or a goat. Whether a player gets the life-long label of being good in the clutch or a choke can be a matter of inches or circumstances. So, I asked Jackie about Don Newcombe.

Don: Jackie, you played ball alongside Don Newcombe during his best years with the Dodgers. Don was a great pitcher, but unfortunately, his accomplishments were clouded by newspaper reporters who claimed that Don couldn't pitch in the clutch. Was there any truth to this?

Jackie: Well, let's go back to the 1951 season that you are talking about. Don pitched two games in one day because we were short of pitchers, you know, a doubleheader. He came in on a very tough situation where we needed a game to win, and he pitched magnificently. Don Newcombe won, I think, 20, what, 25 ball games one year?

Don: Twenty-seven.

Jackie: He won 27 ball games like that. You show me a man that can go out and win 27 ball games during the course of a season and not have guts. I think this gave the newspapermen an opportunity of talking about a guy and gave them a better story – I played with Don; I know him, and if Don didn't have guts, I didn't have any, and I know very well I've got guts.

The statistics bore Jackie Robinson out. On the Saturday night before that 1951 season ended, Don Newcomb pitched nine innings of shutout ball. He beat the Phillies 5-0 for the Dodgers. The next day, Sunday, he pitched the last five innings in relief in the game in which Robinson made that fantastic catch in the bottom of the eleventh inning, and then hit the winning homerun, to save the season for the Dodgers.

Then Newcomb came back on Wednesday for the third and deciding day of the three-game playoff against the Giants. He was pitching with only two days' rest, and he went eight and a third innings before giving way to Ralph Branca. Then he came out, after pitching, with only two days' rest, and after going 14 innings the previous weekend. Years later, newspaper reporters would cite his failure to win the third game of the playoffs with the Giants as an example that he was not a clutch performer.

If Newcombe had had Mariano Rivera as his closer, or if Ralph Branca had gotten the final two outs, Newcombe would be remembered for his clutch performances down the stretch of a tight pennant race.

Following is one more example of how close Newcombe came to being a game-saving hero, only to have it slip from his grasp because of events beyond his control.

In 1950, the Dodgers were one game behind the first-place Phillies on the last day of the season, needing only a win over the Phillies to send the Dodgers and the Phillies into a three-game playoff series. I was in the stands, eight years old. My dad had surprised me by picking me up after Sunday School and driving us the hour trip to Ebbetts Field. For nine innings, Newcombe battled Robin Roberts to a one-to-one tie. In the bottom of the ninth inning, Duke Snider singled to center field with Cal Abrams on second base and nobody out.

As he came around third base, Abrams was waived home by third base coach Milton Stock, perhaps because the Phillies centerfielder Richie Ashburn was not noted for having a strong arm. However, Ashburn got off what he later described as one of the best throws of his career to nail Abrams at home plate by ten feet, and Milton Stock was fired the next day.

Had Stock held Abrams at third base, the Dodgers would have had bases loaded with no outs, and if they then had scored just one run, they would have won the game, earned the right to play the Phillies in a playoff for the chance to go to the World Series, and then Newcombe would have been the hero who had allowed only one run over nine innings in this critical game.

However, Dick Sisler hit a three-run homer for the Phillies in the top of the 10th inning, and the game goes down in the books as another game that Newcomb couldn't win in a clutch situation. Over time, people tend to forget details and just remember the wins and losses that are in the record books.

So how slim is the difference between being labeled a hero or a choke?

Consider this:

If in 1950, Milton Stock holds Cal Abrams at third base and the Dodgers score one run in the ninth inning with the bases loaded and no out, and if the following year Ralph Branca gets two outs instead of giving up a home run to Bobby Thompson, then the record books will show that Don Newcomb was the hero that got the

Dodgers into the playoffs in 1950, and the clutch performer who got them into the World Series in 1951 by pitching a shutout on the last Saturday of the season, throwing 5 2/3 innings of shutout relief the next day, and then allowing only two runs in 8 1/3 innings in the deciding game against the Giants with only two days of rest.

Instead, the record book shows that Newcomb was the losing pitcher in the final critical game in 1950 and failed to win the decisive game in 1951. The details of how well he pitched with so little rest are lost to most people's recollections.

It is indicative of the changes in baseball since 1950 that both Newcombe and Roberts pitched complete nine-inning games on that last day of the 1950 season, in contrast to starting pitchers of today who often pitch only five or six innings and rarely complete a game. In 2022 the major league pitcher with the most complete games was Sandy Alcantara of the Miami Marlins, who pitched all nine innings in five of his 32 starts. By contrast, in 1950 alone, the Phillies' Roberts pitched 30 complete games, and in his nineteen-year career, he went all nine innings 305 times.

To gain even more of a historical perspective, the pitcher with the most career complete games was Cy Young, who retired in 2011, having completed 749 games in which he started. More recently, Warren Spahn retired in 1965 with 382 complete games, and Tom Seaver left baseball in 1986 with 231 complete games credited to his record.

Don Newcombe himself completed 136 games in his ten-year career, including September 6th, 1950, when he nearly pitched two complete games on a day when he started both games of a doubleheader. In the opener, he shut out the Phillies 2-0. In the second game, he was taken out in the 7th inning, having given up only two runs in a game the Dodgers came back to win 3-2.

★★★

PART FOUR: THE NARRATOR MAKES A FOOL OF HIMSELF

Here are some interesting anecdotes, the first of which is, to my eternal embarrassment:

Until recently, I was 100% certain that I had seen Cal Abrams as the potential winning run, trip going around third base, causing him to be thrown out at home plate by ten feet on the last day of the season in 1950. Since I had been in the ball park the day of the game and had seen the play, I had no reason to check my facts until I began writing this book. However, I have now googled every article I could locate about that 1950 end-of-the-season game, and sheepishly I have to admit that I can find no support for this memory which I carried as an eight-year-old for more than 65 years.

Plain and simple, Cal Abrams apparently was thrown out at home plate for three reasons: 1) It was the coach's mistake not to hold him at third base; 2) Ashburn fired a straight as an arrow throw to the catcher; and 3) Ashburn had been moving closer to the infield than he would normally play because the manager had signaled for the pitcher to make a pickoff throw to second base, however, the pitcher missed the signal so when he pitched to Snider, Ashburn the centerfielder was significantly closer to the infield than he would have been. Had he been playing at his usual depth he most likely could not have thrown out Abrams at home plate.

But in the mid-1960s, I was still certain that the Dodgers had lost the 1950 pennant because Abrams had tripped going around third base. Only recently out of college, at the time, I was with friends having a few beers, probably a few too many, in a Garden City, New York bar when I looked at the matches on the table in front of me, and the cover read, "Cal Abrams' Blossom Lounge." Absolutely certain it was just a coincidence that the owner of the 'Blossom Lounge' had the same name as the former ball player, I called, in a rather loud voice, to my friend Joe Covello who was seated opposite me at the other end of a long table, "Hey, Joe, do you think this is the same Cal Abrams who had played for the Dodgers? You know, the bum who tripped over third base in 1950, costing the Dodgers the pennant?"

Joe tried to signal me, but I was too intent on my little joke, or what I thought was a joke, and as I continued to repeat the question, louder each time, I kept ignoring Joe's repeated efforts to get me to shut up. He kept pointing in the direction of the bar, and when I finally shifted my gaze in the direction Joe was pointing, I saw the bartender, who WAS the same Cal Abrams who had played for the Dodgers, leaning with his elbows on the counter, and his chin resting on his hands, just staring at me.

Embarrassed and trying to make a lame joke out of it, I crawled under the table and reached back up for the glass of beer. However, my hand caught the side of the glass, knocking it over and spilling a nearly full glass of beer on the floor next to me. A moment later, there was Cal Abrams standing alongside me, a mop in his hand. He pushed the mop toward me, turned and walked back to the bar, and never said a word.

Here are a few more anecdotes from the Robinson era before we continue with the 1962 interview:

Not only was it uncommon for a ballplayer in Jackie Robinson's era to have a job outside of baseball, but salaries were so low in relation to the overall economy that many ballplayers, except perhaps the marquee names, often held winter jobs to supplement their baseball income. These were the days before Curt Flood's lawsuit led to free agency in the 1970s and ultimately led to the astronomical salaries that many baseball players receive in this day and age.

Reportedly, Hank Greenburg and Jackie Robinson were the only former ball players to stand up for Flood when he sacrificed his career to fight for the right to negotiate with all teams. Flood told Commissioner of Baseball Bowie Kuhn, "I do not regard myself as a piece of property to be bought or sold."

There is one more Cal Abrams story that he told about himself in an article he wrote for *Jewish Major Leaguers in Their Own Words.*

Abrams had been invited to be the featured guest on Happy Felton's Knot Whole Gang, a program that preceded many of the Dodger home games on channel 9 in New York. The players who were the guests on a particular day received $50 and a chance to receive an additional $50. One of their chores was to designate one of three youngsters as the one with the most potential. The youngster so designated would receive $50 and would be asked to designate, in turn, his favorite Dodger player, who would also receive $50. So if the guest Dodger player were named by the youngster as his favorite Dodger player, he would receive $50 for appearing on the show and another $50 for being the youngster's favorite Dodger.

Abrams cornered one of the youngsters before the show and offered to select him if he, in turn, would name Abrams as his favorite player so that Abrams could garner the additional $50. Everything went according to script up to a point. Happy Felton asked Abrams which of the three youngsters he thought had the most potential, and Abrams named the youngster with whom he had plotted. Then Felton asked the chosen young man who his favorite player was, and he promptly said, "Carl Furillo."

One other tale helps to bring us back to a time when baseball club owners decided the salaries of their players, and the players, no matter how successful their season had been, had little leverage and, therefore, had no choice but to accept what they were offered. As a result of the owners having all the leverage in negotiations, salaries were rarely extravagant.

Branch Rickey had been part-owner of the Dodgers from 1942 through 1950, at which time he sold his share in the Dodgers to Walter O'Malley, who subsequently, in 1957, moved the Dodgers from Brooklyn to Los Angeles. Rickey then, in 1950, became general manager of the lowly Pittsburgh Pirates, a team that was a perennial last-place team. While Rickey is lauded for his critical role in Robinson's breaking of the color barrier, not all players shared the love of him that Robinson evinced.

Ralph Kiner, who was to become a Hall of Famer himself, does not recall his experiences with Pirates General Manager Branch Rickey with any degree of fondness, although he speaks of Robinson as "The best athlete ever to play Major League baseball." When speaking of Rickey, Kiner once said, "He was cheap."

As the story goes, Kiner had one of his many outstanding seasons, leading or being close to the lead in home runs and RBIs when he met with Rickey to discuss what he thought would be the significant raise his performance had earned him. Instead, Rickey offered him a cut in pay, and when Kiner cited his statistics and asked why, in light of all he had accomplished, he was not being offered a substantial raise, according to a biographical article about Kiner by Warren Corbett, Rickey's response was, "Son, we could have finished last without you."

★★★

PART FIVE: SPIT BALLS, AND THE BEST CLUTCH HITTERS

My next question was kind of dumb because if a pitcher was throwing a spit ball, certainly the catcher would know about it. However, Jackie responded without hinting at the dubiousness of the question. I said,

Don: Jackie, you played ball alongside Preacher Roe for several years. Preacher was a tremendous pitcher with the Dodgers, but after he retired he admitted in a magazine article that he had thrown a spitball on many occasions. Did you know that he was throwing a spitball while you were playing alongside him? Did any of the Dodgers know that Preacher Roe was throwing a spitball?

Jackie: Well, Campanella certainly had to know because he wouldn't have been able to catch that ball. I see a ball go up and dip, but frankly we didn't know because he didn't tell us and certainly then, if he told us and we started being alert toward it, the umpire would know about it. So although we knew by conversation that Roe was a spitball pitcher at times, just like we knew that there were many other guys in baseball that were spitball pitchers, we didn't know the given pitch that he was going to throw it. It's kind of remarkable that a guy with his cunning and all was able to do the kinds of things that Preacher was. He was a great pitcher and a great competitor.

In August 1920 Ray Chapman was hit in the head by a pitched baseball and became the only major league player ever to die from an on-field injury. That same year the spitball was outlawed with other substance abuse pitches. One of the reasons was that while it was difficult for batters to hit a spitball because of its unpredictable trajectory, for the same reason it could cause injury since it was difficult for pitchers to control. While it might not be correct to attribute the banning of the spitball to the death of Ray Chapman, this may have been one of the reasons that major league baseball ceased using dirty baseballs as well as banning the spitball. Today, it seems that a new clean baseball is put into play after almost every pitch.

Jackie: And as I sit here and talk to you, you know, sit here and have you remember all these statistics and things reminds me of Howard Cosell there in New York. He was the kind of guy who was just the same kind of mind to be able to remember all of these events. You must have a great love for this game of baseball and sports to be able to remember it this way and I find it marvelous to sit here and reminisce with you and listen to you talk about the things that happened. Don Newcomb - 5-0 pitching 5 innings the next day and then come back with two days rest and pitching the way he did. That's remarkable and I'm really enjoying it.

It didn't require any research for me to prepare for this interview. From the time I was eight years old, I had been a die-hard Dodger fan and an ardent Jackie Robinson admirer. I wore his number 42 proudly on my

Dodger jersey and batted with my bat held high, at the level of my right ear, as he did.

For Mother's Day or Mom's birthday at the end of June, my brother Gary and I often gave her a gift of a visit to Ebbetts Field to see the Dodgers. (Of course, our dad was complicit as we surprised Mom with this gift, and he footed the bill.) In the 1950s, as I have mentioned, almost every Dodger game was on the radio, and most were on TV.

Mom and I would watch the games together, and when the Dodgers were behind, it was my job to light a cigarette for her to provide the necessary luck the Dodgers would need to win the game. This seemed to almost always work. Whether it was because of a connection between my lighting of Mom's cigarette and the ability of the Dodger players to hit or because the Dodgers had one of the best hitting teams of all time and were likely to score runs in the late innings with or without our help is for others to decide.

It is curious that about the time my mother gave up smoking in 1957 (and would refrain from cigarettes for the rest of her life), the Dodgers began to encounter a little more difficulty winning as they moved to the West Coast, although with Koufax and Drysdale leading the way, they did win four pennants in the next ten years.

The Dodgers of the 1950s were easy to follow, for they were one of the most exciting teams of all time. Since their pitching was usually a weak spot, they needed to score runs. And for this, they had such great players as Duke Snider, Roy Campanella, Carl Furillo, Gil Hodges, and Peewee Reese. I asked Jackie Robinson,

Don: If you had a choice, which of those players would you like to see up in the clutch, say, in the ninth inning with the bases loaded?

Jackie: Very good question. That is a very good question. There's one guy you left out in there that I have to say I'd like to see up there, Billy Cox. I'd like to see Billy Cox up in a situation like that; then I'd think it would be Jim Gilliam. These are the fellows, I believe, were the same kind of hitters, whether it was 10-0, or 1 to nothing, or two outs with the bases loaded. I like to see the guy who could walk up under any situation and do the same kind of thing. If some fellow who could hit .324 or .320, when that situation arose, they weren't quite the performers that the other guys were, but day in and day out, they would get their base hits and do the kinds of things that make them a standout ballplayer.

But in a clutch situation, Billy Cox, I'd love to see out there because if Billy is going to get a hit he's going to get it. It didn't make any difference, and that's the way I felt about my roommate, Jim Gilliam.

Ironically, third baseman Billy Cox was known for his defensive abilities, and he was an even lighter hitter than Junior Gilliam.

★★★

PART SIX: WHAT'S NEXT, AFTER BASEBALL

Before ending my interview with Jackie Robinson, I wanted to find out his present status and plans for the future. I knew that he was vice president of Chock Full o' Nuts, and I knew that something had happened recently at the company that Robinson had been given an honor or a promotion or something, but I wasn't quite sure. Notice how tactfully Jackie Robinson answered when I incorrectly asked him about the promotion which I thought he had been given but about which I was wrong. I said to Jackie,

Don: That's your current status, correct, you are the vice president of Chock Full o' Nuts, and I think you recently got a promotion, is that right?

Jackie: Well, no, when you go from the vice president to a promotion, that's got to be the presidency, and I haven't been moved up there, and I don't ever expect to. I have been appointed as a member of the board. This may be what you are talking about as far as promotions are concerned, and it was a tremendous honor because I think Chock Full o' Nuts is one of the finest companies around, and to be a member of the board is a big thrill.

Jackie added that the reason he didn't ever expect to be president was that he and everyone else had so much respect for the current president, Mr. Black. Then I asked Jackie the question which had been on my mind throughout our entire interview and which I imagine had been on the minds of almost all baseball fans since Jackie Robinson retired from baseball.

Don: Is there any chance that you'll ever be back in baseball, say, as a manager or coach?

Jackie: No chance, Don. I am very happy at Chock Full o 'Nuts. At one time, Chock Full o 'Nuts was interested in buying the ball club, and we were talking about that, you know, there was a lot of interest. People were asking me what I thought about it. Should we do this, or should we do that? I felt then if they did, it would be a great thing because it would be Chock Full o' Nuts, and I would still be a part of the company. I don't think I could leave a man like William Black to go into another field, whether it's baseball or whether it's another business. I'm very happy and very content with where I am.

PART SEVEN: POLITICS AND CIVIL RIGHTS

Because of his intelligence and because of his ability to express himself, people respect Jackie Robinson's attitude toward politics and his opinions on the political scene. Jackie Robinson was a significant representative of people of color. Therefore, I asked Jackie Robinson,

Don: Why had you come out during the 1960 election campaign so strongly for Richard Nixon? Do you still feel you'd rather have Richard Nixon in the White House, or are you more satisfied with President Kennedy now, or less satisfied than you thought he would be? Exactly how do feel about President Kennedy?

Jackie: Well, there are times that I am very pleased with the Kennedy administration. And then there comes a time like the State of the Union; if you are going to talk about civil rights and then in the press conference someone questions him about the housing bill that he promised to give to the American people, for him to say that he is going to sign this bill when he deems it in the best interest of the public, I have to be disturbed and upset about something like this because it's always the Negro who gets the things last. It's always the Negro who has to be satisfied and contented with conditions as they are. If they anger somebody else, then we're not going to do anything about them. If they're happy with them, then they'll make the decision.

I'm not saying that Mr. Nixon would have done any better. It's a most difficult thing to say, but my feeling is that certainly any President, President Kennedy included, has to be pressed, has to be hit when he makes a mistake, and this is what I believe.

I have no way in the world of saying whether Mr. Nixon would have been a better man. I thought so at the time. If the election was to be run tomorrow and the conditions were the same, and if Mr. Kennedy had said to me as he did in Washington,

"Jack, my trouble is that coming from Boston, I didn't have the chance to know the Negro," I certainly wouldn't support him then because as I looked at the Senator who had been in the Congress and Senate for some 14 years and still did not know the Negro, he couldn't possibly get my support to learn about my people and me in four years.

When I talked to Mr. Nixon, I was convinced he was sincere. He wasn't going out and doing the things I would like to see him do. He wasn't saying things; I think this cost him the election, but he told me confidentially, and people on his staff told me what Mr. Nixon was aiming to do, and the problem is, he said, "We don't think we can get the Negro vote, so therefore, we have got to try to win, but we promise you we are going to do certain kinds of things." And he convinced me of his sincerity.

So I supported him because Mr. Nixon convinced me. I didn't support Senator Kennedy because he told me he didn't know anything about the Negro and somebody who doesn't know anything about us, we are a complicated people and I think that somebody who doesn't know anything about us, it's not right to try to learn about us in four years, especially as the President of the United States.

Don: How about those of us here in the North, Jackie, who believe fervently in the positions the Negro is taking now in the cause, in the sit-in, in strikes down South, and so forth, but who perhaps can't participate as Reverend Martin Luther King suggested, in a protest march down to Georgia or perhaps don't have enough money to contribute to the NAACP. Is there anything that people like this can do to help the Negro cause and to make themselves heard?

Jackie: Certainly. You know, there are protests, people can stand up and be counted when certain issues are made. You don't have to go south. I don't go South and participate in the sit-ins because the kids down there said don't come down because we don't want any of the people down here saying those Northern agitators are down here again. We're going to do this thing. What we need is your moral and financial support, but don't let it be known that you're coming down here participating, leading a movement. We want the people in the South to do this kind of thing. So what I've done is give them every bit of moral support. I let them know that I believe enough in America. These youngsters ought to continue to press for their rights here in their country. And I think that most Americans ought to do this.

As I see it, most of the Northerners have not been affected to the point that they want to participate. They believe with the people down there, and they say, "Gee whiz, this isn't right," but they haven't really been touched by it. They haven't been affected, so they sit, and they look as they see it happen and read a newspaper, and they really feel sorry and feel bad about it, but when they stand up one of these days and say, "You know, I'm going to do something about it; I'm going to write to my Congressman. I'm going to let him know they have to do something about this kind of thing," then you're doing something. It doesn't take actual participation, in my opinion. It takes interest, and it does take a letter here and there keeping up with the events and letting people know exactly how you feel.

***

Here are some quotes from Jackie Robinson about civil rights and human dignity:

"The right of every American to first-class citizenship is the most important issue of our time."

"I don't think that I or any other Negro, as an American citizen, should have to ask for anything that is rightfully his. We are demanding that we just

be given the things that are rightfully ours and that we are not looking for anything else."

"Since participation in a democracy is dependent on basic freedoms that everyone else takes for granted, we need to make no apologies for being especially interested in catching up on civil rights."

"Civil rights is not by any means the only issue that concerns me, nor I think, any other Negro. As Americans, we have as much at stake in this country as anyone else."

"Negros aren't seeking anything which is not good for the Nation as well as ourselves. In order for America to be 100% strong economically, defensively, and morally, we cannot afford the waste of having second and third-class citizens."

"I believe in the goodness of our free society, and I believe a society can remain good only as long as *we are willing to fight for it and to fight against whatever imperfections may exist."*

"I won't have it made until the most underprivileged Negro in Mississippi can live in equal dignity with anyone else in America."

PART EIGHT: ROBINSON REMINISCES

I had wanted to ask Jackie Robinson if by staying out of baseball, he did not think he was being unfair to his many fans, to the fans who would come out to the park just to watch Jackie Robinson in perhaps a coaching capacity, or even just sitting on the bench alongside the players.

I had wanted to ask Jackie Robinson if he didn't feel he owed it to baseball to stay in the sport as long as possible. However, after he answered my next question, I realized that there was no need to ask Jackie Robinson why he didn't feel he owed anything to baseball and why he didn't return. His next answer satisfied me on all these points.

The question I had asked Jackie Robinson to conclude my once-in-a-lifetime interview was,

Don: What are the things you most remember about your ten years in the sport?

Jackie: Well, Don, I'd have to put it this way. You know I have a beautiful home in Stamford, Connecticut. I sit in my dining room, and I look out through our picture window, and I look at the land that I have around, and I think, had it not been for baseball, I couldn't have this.

I look at the things my children have that I didn't have; had it not been for baseball, all these things could not have been. I look at the things that my wife is doing, the kinds of jobs that she's attempted to do in the community, working with people working at the hospital as a psychiatric nurse because she loves it. Had it not been for baseball, she wouldn't be able to devote this kind of time to the things that she is interested in.

So, what else could I say other than the fact that as I look back at baseball, I thank baseball from the bottom of my heart for all it has done? I sincerely believe that although I loved it and that I look back on it with great love and care, and appreciation, I don't want to look back to the point to say I got to run back into baseball and participate.

I am not one to look back in this respect. But I am grateful. I certainly remember the many great things that I've had. I remember Ebbetts Field. I listened to the wonderful fans there and went back even further when I was in Montreal when I was up there and the way the fans reacted to me.

I've got so many fond memories, Don, that I could sit here for the rest of your tape and talk about the many wonderful people who have contributed to where I am and as I am here in Boston to be a part of the Boston Writers' Dinner, I can just be thankful to God and all of the wonderful people who have helped me through the years because I look back, seventeen years ago, and I ask myself, do you remember whether or not you will be able to get your next meal soon, 17 years ago.

So baseball has given me a lot that I would never have been able to get. I'm grateful. I'm appreciative. It has enabled me to come up and have this wonderful chat with you; had it not been for baseball, all these things could not have been.

It has now been more than 75 years since Jackie Robinson broke the color barrier in baseball and won the first Rookie of the Year award for his performance in 1947. Our country has recognized the historical significance of this, and professional baseball has honored him by retiring his number 42 and not allowing any future player to wear that number. In 1986, Robinson, who died in 1972, was posthumously awarded the highest civilian honor: The Medal of Freedom was accepted by his wife, Rachel, on behalf of her late husband and presented by the then president, Ronald Reagan.

During the 1997 baseball season, 50 years after his major league debut, there were festivities and celebrations of Robinson's feats in every ballpark across the United States and in Canada. Yet, in the current environment where the media rushes to go public with the slightest bit of rumored scandal about anyone of celebrity status, I have not seen one ill word about Jackie Robinson's personal or professional life. My childhood idol was not only an exemplary athlete and a heroic figure in the battle for equal rights, but – as a person – he was a wonderful role model for me and so many others.

Don: Well, thank you very much, Jackie Robinson, and for the privilege of having this chat with you, I am grateful to baseball.

Jackie: Thank you very much.

★★★

PART NINE: Quotes From and About Jackie Robinson

I will conclude this book with some additional quotes about and from Jackie Robinson.

Jackie Robinson, speaking of Willie Mays, possibly the greatest all-around player to ever play the game and certainly one of the most popular:

"When he was in California, whites refused to sell him a house in their community. They loved his talent, but they didn't want him for a neighbor."

Willie Mays speaking of Jackie Robinson:

"Every time I look at my pocketbook, I see Jackie Robinson."

Sports writer Milton Gross:

"They call his name in the way no other player's name is called. They plead to shake his hand or ask for his autograph. They touch his clothes as he walks by, unhurrying, pleasant, friendly, cooperative, because Jackie has never lost sight of what the game has meant to him, and what he has meant, means now, and will always mean to his people."

Charlie Dressen, who managed the Dodgers from 1951 through 1953:

"Give me 5 players like (Jackie) Robinson and a pitcher and I'll beat any nine man team in baseball."

Mickey Mantle spoke of Robinson after the Yankees beat the Dodgers in the seventh and final game of the 1952 World Series:

"After the Series, he came into our clubhouse and shook my hand. "You're a helluva ballplayer," he

said. I thought, "Man, what a class guy. I never could have done that, not in a million years. I'm a really bad loser. And he told the press that I was the difference and that the Yankees didn't even miss Joe DiMaggio, who had retired the year before. I have to admit I became a Jackie Robinson fan on the spot. And when I think of that World Series, his gesture is what comes to mind. Here was a player who had, without doubt suffered more abuse and more taunts and more hatred than any player in the history of the game. And he had made a special effort to compliment and encourage a young white kid from Oklahoma."

Robinson's fellow teammate, shortstop Peewee Reese, also in the Hall of Fame, was a Southerner born and raised in Kentucky who famously sent a message to the country in front of a stadium packed with fans when he walked from his position at shortstop to stand beside Robinson who was playing second base, According to Reese:

"To do what he did has got to be the most tremendous thing I've ever seen in sports. Thinking about the things that happened, I don't know any other ball player who could have done what Jackie Robinson did. To be able to hit with everybody yelling at him. He had to block all that out, block out everything but this ball that is coming in at a hundred miles an hour and he's got a split second to make up his mind if it's in or out or down or coming at his head, a split second to swing. To do what he did has got to be the most tremendous thing I've ever seen in sports."

Branch Rickey, the Dodger owner, identified Robinson as the person to accept the challenge of what Robinson labeled "The Rickey Experiment." Rickey called Robinson, "a credit to baseball and a credit to America."

Authors Truman K. Gibson Jr. & Steve Huntley, in their book *Knocking Down Barriers: My Fight for Black America,* write:

"*When he joined the major leagues, Jackie said he made it clear to baseball owner Branch Rickey that he would not suffer physical attack. 'I told Mr. Rickey that if a pitcher hits me intentionally, his ass belongs to me. And if a second baseman strikes me intentionally, his ass belongs to me. Apparently the warning was passed down the line. When we went to St. Louis and faced the gashouse gang, the pitcher Burley threw a fastball that hit me,' Jackie recalled. 'I lay my bat down and started toward the pitcher. He said, "God Jackie, I didn't mean that!" So the word got down the league. They called me names, but I expected those. But nobody hit me intentionally.'*"

Civil Rights Leader Jesse Jackson:

"*He was a therapist for the masses by succeeding, by doing it with such style, flair and drama. He helped level baseball off, to make it truly a game of black and white, with excellence the only test for success. When Jackie took the field, something reminded us of our birthright to be free."*

Robinson's fellow teammate, centerfielder Duke Snider, also in the Hall of Fame:

"He knew he had to do well. He knew that the future of blacks in baseball depended on it. The pressure was enormous, overwhelming, and unbearable at times. I don't know how he held up. I know I never could have."

Snider added:

"Jackie Robinson was the greatest competitor I've ever seen. I've seen him beat a team with his bat, his ball, his glove, his feet and, in a game in Chicago one time, with his mouth."

Gene Butig, President of the American League 1994-1997:

"He led the Nation by example. He reminded our people of what was right and he reminded them of what was wrong. I think it can safely be said today that Jackie Robinson made the United States a better Nation."

President Ronald Reagan:

"He struck a mighty blow for equality, freedom and the American way of life. Jackie Robinson was a good citizen, a great man, and a true American champion."

St. Louis Cardinal Hall of Fame Pitcher Bob Gibson:

"If I were in Jackie Robinson's shoes, I probably never would have made it. He's a hero. My hero."

Author Roger Kahn of *The Boys of Summer* about the Brooklyn Dodgers:

"Jackie Robinson made his country and you and me and all of us a shade more free. Robinson did not merely play at center stage. He was center stage; and wherever he walked, center stage moved with him. He bore the burden of a pioneer and the weight made him strong. If one can be certain of anything in baseball, it is that we shall not look upon his like again."

Hank Aaron, Hall of Fame outfielder and record holder for most career home runs:

"Jackie's character was much more important than his batting average."

Dr. Martin Luther King Jr.:

"Jackie Robinson made my success possible. Without him, I would never have been able to do what I did."

And some additional quotes attributed to Jackie Robinson himself:

"Many people resented my impatience and honesty, but I never cared about acceptance as much as I cared about respect."

"Plenty of times I wanted to haul off when somebody insulted me for the color of my skin, but I had to hold to myself. I knew I was kind of an experiment. The whole thing was bigger than me."

"I think if we go back and check our record, the Negro has proven beyond a doubt that we have been more than patient in seeking our rights as American citizens."

"There's not an American in this country free until every one of us is free."

"Life is not a spectator sport. If you're going to spend your whole life in the grandstand just watching what goes on, in my opinion you're wasting your life."

"I'm not concerned with your liking or disliking me… all I ask is that you respect me as a human being."

We will conclude with a quote attributed to Jackie Robinson that I try to use as a guide for my own life. Jackie once said:

"A life is not important except in the impact it has on other lives."

If that indeed is the measure of a person, then is there any denying that Jackie Robinson's life was, by his own standard, important?

About The Author

Don Mesibov is the author and coauthor of five books, four of which are focused on the education field. His most recent, published this past June, is entitled, "Helping Students Take Control of Their Own Learning." A memoir, published in 2010, focused on the last nine months of his mother's life when, in the advanced stages of Alzheimer's, Don, and his wife Susan and their two daughters, brought her to live with them; their son, out of the nest, frequently visited.

Upon graduation from Boston University with a degree in communications/public relations, Don went to work at the checkout counter of the Star Market in Brookline, Massachusetts. "I wanted to raise money to buy an overnight summer camp," he explained, "but I had no funds of my own; so I earned enough at the super market to live on, and I travelled weekends trying to locate investors. Although I ultimately failed to raise sufficient funding, the experience getting to know people in a different context has served me well through life," he says.

Don works as an educational consultant, training teachers to actively engage students in the learning process. During a varied career he has worked as a door-to-door encyclopedia salesman; a summer camp counselor, then athletic director; a child-care counselor at a school for children with special needs; a reporter, then editor, of a weekly newspaper; a teachers' union labor relations specialist; and for the past 28 years he has been director of The Institute for Learning Centered Education, an organization he founded.

His current focus is on an autism initiative he has launched to train school staff and public organization leaders to understand how to provide services and support for people on the spectrum and their families. He welcomes the involvement of anyone with an interest in autism to contact him at demesibov@gmail.com

Don is an avid gardener with 175 flower gardens at his home in Potsdam, New York, near the Canadian border. His wife Susan tends to nine raised beds which provide food for the summer as well as products that can be frozen and partaken during the long, cold Potsdam winters. "Our father, and grandfather (mine and Gary's), each died of heart attacks at the age of 52, so I have always been aware of the need to exercise. When I was younger," Don continues, "I would run a lot, but I found running in circles to be exceedingly boring. However, I can get out in the gardens at 8 am and still be working, and enjoying it, when Susan yells from the house, "Don't you know it's getting dark?"

ACKNOWLEDGEMENTS

To nephews Brian and Todd, their wives Sally and Katie, and to their children Anna and Claire, and Eleanor and Milo. And to my granddaughters Avery, Emelia, Madelyn, and Julia. You are all such wonderful people with strong character and warm personalities which makes the lives of Laurie and Gary ever meaningful. Their careers of caring for others set them apart, and their legacy is magnified by the lives you are each leading.

To: cousins Gail and Fred who were more like siblings to Gary and me. Fred passed much too soon, but Gail remains an inspiration and more like a sister than cousin.

To all of the self-sacrificing people who have worked with me on our Institute and now on our Autism Initiative. The opportunity to work with quality people like you and my family is what has made my journey through life worthwhile.

To Larry Byrd (B Y R D, not the basketball player, B I R D). For those who knew Larry Byrd no explanation is necessary; and for those who didn't have the privilege of knowing him, no amount of words will do.

And to all those who recognize that our own true happiness can only come from trying to bring happiness to others and by doing our best to always do what we know to be right.

And finally, *I acknowledge those who, recognizing my complete lack of ability with anything of a technological nature, have mercifully come to my rescue time and again:*

My wife Susan and my children Raina, Marli, and Darren who in-person, or walking me through each step of the way, would bail me out when the button I pushed on my computer would not bring about the anticipated result.

BOOKS BY AUTHOR DON MESIBOV

Mesibov, Schopler, and TEACCH: Changing the World for Parents, and People with Autism From Refrigerator Mothers to Treating Parents as Partners (Mesibov, 2022, Elite Authors)

Helping students Take Control of their Own Learning – 279 Learner-Centered, Social Emotional Strategies for Teachers (Mesibov and Drmacich, 2022, Routledge, Taylor and Frances Group)

Appreciating Mom through The Lens of Alzheimer's – A Care Giver's Story (Mesibov, 2014, Create Space)

Captivating Classes with Constructivism (Flynn, Mesibov, Vermette, Smith, 2013, Rainmaker Education)

Applying Standards-Based Constructivism: A Two-Step Guide for Motivating Elementary Students (Flynn, Mesibov, Vermette, Smith, 2004, Eye on Education)

Applying Standards-Based Constructivism: A Two-Step Guide for Motivating Middle and High School Students (Flynn, Mesibov, Vermette, Smith, 2004, Eye on Education)

CREDITS

Sam and Gail Gold of Sam Gold Video who spent countless hours working with me on my narrative and improving the sound quality of the reel-to-reel taped interview of Jackie Robinson.

William Eckert, Director of Adult Services, Potsdam Public Library, Potsdam, New York, who volunteered his time and equipment to record this final version of the audiobook.

Made in the USA
Middletown, DE
15 October 2023

40774547R00062